Left Wanting More

Poems by

Marc J. LaFountain

Ⱶ

Vabella Publishing
P.O. Box 1052
Carrollton, Georgia 30112
www.vabella.com

Copyright © 2015 Marc J. LaFountain

The cover art is a 1973 watercolor by the author entitled "Dancer."

Manufactured in the United States of America

Library of Congress Control Number: 2015918523

13-digit ISBN 978-1-938230-94-3

10 9 8 7 6 5 4 3 2 1

For my father, Robert,
the first poet I ever knew

Contents

Nature/Identity

Keeping is not Keeping

i am the keeper of the blades
of grass, their green vitality
my charge.

i rescue from the cats the sweet
little ring neck snake,
so docile and gentle, yet ever
so determined, so writhing with
diminutive ferocity.

i am the keeper of the earthworm,
wrongly scooped into a pail of hot
blue gravel hostile to its life.

delivering it to nearby kin in the old pump house,
i am the keeper of the baby deer mouse,
eyes not yet fully open, shivering,
its little legs grasping and clinging,
plundered from its nest on a freezing night
by a marauding young panther.

i levitate stones and dirt,
float on their surfaces,
and so become a gem,
or maybe the crystal that
could become a gem.

for a young boy i grow a hat
under a tree.

i am the keeper of the scent
of old heart pine,
of the sensuousness of maple and fir.

Corwith Avenue

My bed was nestled by the great holly
in a small hedge-rimmed courtyard next to
the old shingled house whose chimney
was a trumpetvine trellis and whose
cellar window channeled streams
of coal that tamed the winter.

Under a quilt of leaves orange, red and yellow
stitched by my mother's mother,
I laid on my back watching
silent snow fall everywhere,
but never on me, for
an arcane canopy magically
stripped the flakes of their time
and their mission, substituting
in their place my concealed
dwelling among them,
my destiny as a double agent for
the visible and the invisible.

Being simple

I once lived in a norman
rockwell town, unaware it
was also peyton's stepford place.

I watched sunbeams flow down
through the clouds in vaporous streams,
knowing them in reverse as watery columns
of the earth's lymph
being taken up into the sky
by some distant draw.

You see, I was naive, so they said.

Nature's child, how could I be but?

What they knew not was that
deep in the woods,
beyond all silly importance,
beyond the streams and
holes of quickmud,
I would lay in a tiny cedar forest
on its soft, rust-colored needles and
gaze at the speckled rays of sky
making their way down the
fragrant canopy.
I would fly up to meet them,
be absorbed in the radiant air.
In silent, dumb joy I would disappear
into some distant draw.

How naive is that?

Agnostic Archer

The little archer formed
a tiny, sharp arrow from
a pithy spirea stalk into which
he had inserted one of his
mother's sewing needles.

Propelled by an equally tiny
bow that had once been a
curved stem holding a chestnut,
strung now with his mother's
sewing thread,

the arrow glanced awkwardly off
a brown shingle on the side of
his family's farmhouse,

letting escape the fly he had made
his quarry,

provoking a painfully long,
frustratingly futile search for his
wee missile,

eventually leading him to ask
of God if he were so great,
so omniscient,
why could he not find his arrow?
why? how simple could a plea be?

Resigned first to prayer, then to
defiant provocation, his unrelenting
interrogation yielded only
stillborn silence.

Perhaps tracing the alchemical arc of
some ancient shadow or primal force
that made of him a hunter,
or the perennial seeker,
the little archer had launched a
barbed query toward the
edge of the unknown, wondering
if it would return, as was promised
in his father's books.

It was clear he was not Longfellow's bowman,
whose arrow, like his song, did return one day.

In the mute lull of his wait
he was touched by
Great Overwhelming Doubt,
and so became the skeptic.

Dining at the St. George Cut

Everything is eating everything else.

Little fish are tasted by larger versions,
and they, unwarned, by diving terns
and pelicans.
Quick stepping plovers and sandpipers snap up
whatever scurries.

Seeking delectable innards, worms drill shells,
conchs scour algaed boulders,
those boulders gobbling the skin
of clumsy climbers.
Rising tides consume the shallow bay.
Oblivious to prior carnage,
shell hunters delight in the skeletal homes
of flesh long since ravaged.

Bravado, hulk hogan-mustachioed fisherman,
who knows everything, rants
about regulations, tossing his lit cigar
into the living water, ruining its purity
and my sanity with his bluster's appetite.

As fall digests the last of summer,
one lone monarch departs
for the open sea,
both devoured by
the horizon.

I swallow the spectacle, myself a tidbit for time.

Ice Storm

limbs surrender
bowed boughs break,
crashing cracking crystal
needles' sleeves shed
pine scented air,
sweet spoils of a
cold carnage.

forsaking heaven in the havoc,
genuflecting hemlocks'
bent branches
face down to grounds once
risen above,
their declining arcs homage
to a slippery silence.

earlier an upright solar bound canopy,
sleet burdened birches' branches
splayed sideways now,
dancer headfirst in the dirt,
legs open to the sky,
acrobatics gone awry.

glazed gusted
frozen fronds
jingle clink,
wind chimes,
death rattles.

Winter Illness, Cold

mired in disconnection in the unwanted
absence of the groove where
time's pace matters,
sequestered from the breezes that whip
and sift distant pines,
my mind hovers, wonderless.

washing undone, calls unreturned,
people ignored, though not forgotten,
presents unwrapped,
things that count no longer do.

no sorcery to animate this still body,
astray even of its astral mooring,
languishing without nostalgia,
a voyeur with blank desire.

there is no magic these days when
nothing descends like the snow that shrouds
the creek secret in the woods,
and me, its brother,
walled in this room.

Desire

Passion

your graceful flow makes of me
rhymes not before moved,
makes this blushing strength
tremble when i see you
lying on your back,
eyes gentle willing,
arms folded back where
all that is soft is
open to me, for me.

down sweet skies
along primal paths,
i fall far into you,
flesh claiming its
animal destiny,
and sigh, longing again
for that radiant place
that poses me once more
to hover,
to trace my disappearance
in your scent.

Once, Once was Not

once i touched you and
you bloomed in luscious fragrance
in a spring that seemed endless.

once you smiled at my hands
wandering aimlessly over your lands,
greeting them, sending out yours.

once my scent,
my contours,
drew you near,
and there was time.

once, once was not.

we were a circle when
passion colored the sky,
i, water for your desiccated lips,
you, you said, the filly
on which i brought it.

Love and Breath

i breathe you in,
honey for my veins.
i breathe you out,
tender vapors for the sky.

in breathe you in,
acid witch curdling colored melodies.
i breathe you out,
fire in the air.

i breathe you in,
balm for my soul.
i breathe you out,
snow's fragrance.

i breathe you in,
it turns me inside out.
i breathe you out
to hasten your return.

i breathe you in
to breathe.
i breathe you out
to breathe.

To See Desire

In dark houses restless media
flicker on blank walls
for fervent blank stares,
for gypsies wandering in dim spaces.

In other houses all lamps are lit
in deaf defiance of entropy,
by fools,
who claim to see better in the light.

Lottery

Rude to the odds and
surly to statistics,
I wish for a fate at least
as good as being struck by
an asteroid or an itinerant hippo,
or even being crushed by a vending machine.

I hope Nietzsche was wrong about
the Eternal Return.

Astride chance and
the fantasy of fantasy,
I toss green to the yon beyond,
and wait.

Left Wanting More

is not always a bad thing.

The common dream though
is to not be left this way.

On a fair day it could be said
something was good, maybe even fine,
which is not to imply
it was incomplete
or insufficient.

Even when it is extraordinary,
you could still be left wanting more,

not to fill a gaping lack, but to
grow older in the vivid presence of
already dreamed of but yet
unborn phantoms,

to open a hint or promise of
a journey somewhere else,

someplace marvelous where
sunflowers ascend blue winds
and pierce the firmament of the banal
that so dampens delight and surprise
in favor of the unfinished and the dismal same
that truly do leave you,
in the worst way,
wanting more.

Quirks & Warps

Afternoon in a Fellini Film with Beau
Bravo and Buddha

Sitting in silence in a meadow yesterday,
a butterfly lit on me for a spell.

Today, in the plaza of the great Metropolitan,
having just seen Klee and on the way
to see Degas and the Egyptians,
an old woman from some
cabaret or carnival of yesteryear,
with exaggerated rouge,
copious red lipstick, a brown mole
on her cheek and raven hair,
and her beagle, old and lame
(not so much by chance),
came to sit beside me in
my silence.

She called him Beau Bravo.
She said he was beautiful.
She spoke to him and cared for him.
She said she could not have treated
her own child better.
She picked him up, put him down,
continually arranging his position.
She tainted him with anxiety,
complicating his hobbled body.

She put her finger in to clean his ear,
wiped it on his coat, which she
also said was beautiful.
She lifted his ears to show me they
were immaculate.
I sat in silence.
She said she cooked for him.
He must be a very happy dog I offered.

She placed him between us and
she too moved nearer.
I sat in silence.
Beau Bravo drooled on her dress.
He ran to a nearby pool, she in pursuit,
shrieking for his return.
Then she abruptly departed,
walking around the corner of a wall
to disappear.
Momentarily she reappeared, impishly
showing only her head from behind the edge.
She gazed at me alluringly.
She sang some ragged notes for me,
serious intent in her eyes.

I sat in silence.
She took leave.

Was far better a dog than a child,
or me, to keep her company,
though I was overcome with compassion
for Beau Bravo.

I sat in silence.
Today there were no butterflies.

Or were there?

A Surrealist Walks into a Grocery Store...

twisted metal glass,
broken cans and
garbage bleeding
in dull colorless air.

lumpy proletarian shoppers
clutch their children
and their wretched eggs
with swollen resignation.

could they become
the surreal marvelous?
might they elevate?
alchemize their obsequious tinfoil?

or are they just that way,
the stinking gravity of
sterile possibility?

pitiful alienation from
alienation, their wings caught in
I Scream.

yes, they have no badada!

Busyness

Next to me at this formerly
quiet table in this serene library
is what appears to be a very busy
business man.

He rattles and tidies his papers,
shuffles them endlessly,
perhaps fortuitously,
impatiently moving about his stacks,
his scribbling pen scratching.

He sighs often, jerks around
without grace, though with
great conviction.
He is hurried, commotion is considerable.

He is at least important,
perhaps powerful,
surely a spectacle.

His shirt is tidy and stiff,
his suspenders impeccable,
his hairs shiny in discrete rows.

He reads about investments in journals,
pamphlets, reports, folders,
fat books.

I, suffering in patience,
contemplate several versions
of the imaginary and ponder
the vividly close yet
infinitely distant present,

and my place somewhere there.

He is figuring the future.
I, becoming a corpse,
am resisting resembling myself.

Which of us, I wonder, is alive?

Romance of the Cliche

there was a time when
merry-go-rounds were magical,
but i have since fallen dunce.

help! i'm trending in the big
reveal,
or fail,
wallowing in the trite.
look, i've fallen and i
can't get up and i
can't find the beef.

i need to ramp it up,
just do it,
you know, leverage it,
stand up and deliver,
put my best foot forward and
break a leg.

wearing a green velvet jacket
trimmed in gold,
with my heart on my sleeve sweating
blood,
i will poke fate in the eye with
my sharp stick,
throw it under the bus
and dance on its grave.

then, with my rose colored glasses,
i will see a silver lining,
but only if it's not all smoke
and mirrors or some can
of worms where i am
all thumbs and thick
as a brick.

Rapture

only the sensitive
walk about
from room to room,
upon the air they see,
emotions out of skin,
kicking, dancing on its surface

white silver spaces long,
round membraned circles
flash in front of eyes

pointed tinsel shimmer sounds
amorphous forms afleeting
in periphery

a journey nondimensional with
continuity illusory

Recipe

The barest of essentials,
the fewest necessary ingredients,
the sparsest of details,
the simplest pieces of a scaffold:

a skeleton for an event

that assumes and concocts
a kind of knowing of
the tricks of heat, moisture, and time,
the vagaries of weight and volume,
and other quirks that can only be
stumbled upon,

a kind of knowing not presumptuous
about results, rather a way
of figuring, of moving,
where consumables fall out
as vestiges of hoping and
venturing into what unfolds,

carried on later as variously contrived rituals
and plots, too many claiming to be
the holy way.

Trying to maintain

Plied in along with all the other
trivial weighty flighty
vexing clutter in my mind,

I got poems in my head
paintings in my head

my head is incandescent,
lucid words shimmering, slipping,
disappearing in fits of starts and fragments,
some whole, some anomalous,
some breech born,
oblique and muffled,
fantasia all in vivid hues and
lurid tints.

No wonder I can't remember
to buy vacuum bags!

Burdens

Child without a Child

the mower turns and severed
leaves of grass fly.
the bird house where once
bluebirds peered at me with wary eyes
is empty now.

i am the last of a generation
the end of a line
a vanishing point
a blank fired into the belly of evolution.

it is August, hot.
the birds have gone.
regret blooms melancholy
in the sky in front of me,
wrenching my body to
some ancient echo that
will never see its day or
become a song.

The Deadening

Wiggling and squirming
to escape the dread,
I scurry from space to space
to hide from the dribble that
sours my senses.

Out on the earth violet
periwinkles tell me I am safe there,
there is no chatter,
no glum faces,
no numbing games.

First here, then there,
the deadening slowly swarms,
water running downhill
assaulting every dry place
in its path.

The Face of the Suffering

what trajectory is this haunting
that sometimes i am so
overwhelmingly sad i
cannot even be angered
when i see their dripping eyes?

the road
i rode,
i, road,

orange fire
luminous vaporous smoke.

passed a man bleeding
in the street

no one looked back.

The Unseen Among the Unstable

Walk a tightrope strung between broken
eggshells scattering like dandelion fairies
in winds perilous and erratic,
winds which drive the inner time of
a primal narcissism, whose absorption,
above all, is manifestation,
regardless.

Here travels a reversal where
invisibility is the curse of the normal,
appropriated to support the wiles of
those whose raw is unfettered,
making for them a world more possible.

In this arrogation the unafflicted
are bruised and bent, carrying on the
backs of their souls the gravity of
those who sink in dark places,

and the concealed carriages they ferry
them upon,
no affirmation of, no compassion accorded
their tormented share.

Narcissus (He had no choice after all)

Each day we ebb a little more
the more we hone imperfection,
clipping away of a piece of skin,
filing or sanding or cutting some
living surface,
rubbing it away,
pulling it out,
wearing it down,
making it go away,

picking at it til it bleeds,
spilling out the within,

sometimes curiously,
maybe hopefully,
just to see,

cloistered, withering
in the calling of being these selves,

dysappearing as we disappear in
one long farewell,

all the while sharing less,
nurturing less,
forsaking the gift of touch,
dissipating the bodies that sustain
like so many hangnails or callouses
to be shed to become
the fervently desired.

Loss

Dad, Oblivious (?) to His Alzheimer's

Doing well, thank you, he said,
nose dripping on mucousy fingers
feeding his chocolate lips.

Meticulously folded tissues obsessively
placed in rows on his table wait their turn,
if ever, to blot that glistening slipperiness.

His pillowy feet, swollen to the knees,
glow bright angry red, shiny,
on the brink of implosion.

Fetid green urine swells
the external bladder that hangs
sideways on his flimsy, bowed leg.

Buttons on his shirt, fidgeted with
for hours, fastened way out of order,
awkwardly pull his dapper shirt over
his hunched shoulders,
making them disappear.

A white pill, unswallowed by his mouth,
for his heart,
lies on his green chair.

Doing well, thank you, he says,
doing well.

What deceit feigns wellness?
What spirit dwells tangled in
this ganglic fog?

Obituaries

scribbles traced on a slippery slide,
spray and sparks of the whirling
wheel that flings off the living,
one by one,
sometimes in clusters.

Spins them off unceremoniously,
always without intent, despite
thick words named to assign design.

Some anonymous, to whom I nod, or not,
some acquaintances who shift my flow,
some so close I gasp at the unfathomable
shuddering my organs, calling out my time,
a moth for fire.

Save in me the amorphous quivering,
the doleful sympathy arising from
below within, there is no notice or dirge
for the dead brown dog, ribs
sticking up in the cold wet grass
by the edge of the road.

Coco Chihuahua

By the old stone wall
one last zinnia has escaped
the night cold, whose
morning frost bejewelled
red hawthorn berries.

At the pond's edge bathing bluejays
spy a single willow leaf
tumbling into the opaque,
where time's portion vanishes,
furrowing memories deep and long.

In the fall
the quick turn still
and go home quietly.

Silent Knight, Christmas in the Nursing
        Home with Ray

Through his door,
on which hangs a sign proclaiming him
the proud grandpa of an army soldier,
he shuffles speechless in tiny, slow steps,
each measured by increasing insufficiency,
toward the sofa in the living room,
toward the fire light,
in demented parkinsonian haze.

He slumbers, shriveling
now a fetal curl teetering
on the rim of some abyss,
lullabyed, coincidentally,
or not,
by the sweet carol's plea:
sleep, in heavenly peace.

Sophie

when the colored leaves came down,
when the sap went down,
the little white dog went down.
down into the ground.
with her i went down,
Down.

in the fall's chill the
warmth that once animated her
rises now white mist over
a cold pond, evaporating,
vanishing.

strung out stunned in desolate air,
my sorrow an aching monument alight
for one Fragmented Moment when,
through the trees' limbs'
slicing shadows,
a glowing slant of sun
falls on the white stone
marking her now.

so deep the numb
all figuring delayed, futile,
mired in dumb feeling,
miasma of muted sadness.

emotions, first murmurs from
a cavernous opening,
hesitantly take names,

become words:
filaments defying
the unspeakable, and

the first rains and fires Since
did not salve,
and still each encounter with a
first-this-or-that
tumbles me forlorn.

saturated in her absence,
i drift,
figment of what i was
when the Sophie dog was here.

lamentable or fortuitous,
there are in each life
but a scant scattering of
pure loves.

little dog, you were one.
i gathered those days sweet
as they were gossamer.

Father's Fleece Shirt Jacket

Not my style at all,
would not have chosen it,
but it choose me.

Soft fabric feigning a rugged exterior,
yet smoothly woven inside,
color of a fawn,
buttons of boney wood,
loose, long, fashionably baggy.

Something not to be worn
in public or in the presence
of those who scorn the
loose and droopy,

yet something so snug
in which to wrap my body when
all about is chill and shiver.

Artifact of a life
whose bearings
were being shifted
by old age,
a forgetfulness
of time and space,

of a body whose familiar routes were
now all tangles,

non-sequiturs

of a life whose objects
now fit several suitcases,
some boxes and bags.

Given me in his absence,
the last thing I would have
thought of then already reeling
dazed from culling among his things
those to disappear forever
into some anonymous charity.

Already sensing futures,
anticipating torrents of memories,
of spectral visitations,
I pulled it into my orbit.

Days would come when I would slip
inside this magic cloak,

into the scent of the talc
left when he was younger and
wore my bathrobe on his visits,

into the scent of the aftershave on my shirt
from when he hugged me goodbye,

into that place where a core glows
steady, radiating into all around it,

where I am bathed in the
sweet warmth only nostalgia brings
when it arrives splendidly, that is,
not draped in melancholy,

or if so, a melancholy
so soothing,
so joyfully numbing,
transporting.

Marc J LaFountain, born in Massachusetts, grew up on the east end of Long Island. After receiving his PhD in Sociology from the University of Tennessee, he taught at several universities before joining the University of West Georgia in 1977. He retired from there in 2008 and continues to live in Carrollton with his wife, Sharon, where he pursues a passion for the conservation of native plants. Their children, Nic and Dante, live in the Atlanta area. A painter as well as writer, his poems are strong on visual imagery and are colored by romanticism, symbolism, expressionism and surrealism. In addition to various academic publications, he is also the author of *Dali and Postmodernism: This is Not an Essence* (SUNY Press). Fascinated by the oblique and the elliptical, his subject matter ranges from everyday observations to commentaries on the banal to poignant encounters with his Dad's Alzheimers.

www.ingramcontent.com/pod-product-compliance
Lightning Source LLC
Chambersburg PA
CBHW061159040426
42445CB00013B/1737